D0386022

49589

LC
148
.W54

Williams, William G.
Enrollment Strategy.

DATE DUE		
OCT 21 1985		
APR 2 5 1988		
NOV 20 1989		
MAY 5 1995		

Pennsylvania College of Technology

Formerly The Williamsport Area Community College

GE

PENNSTATE

1855

ENROLLMENT STRATEGY

102 Suggestions
for Enrollment Success
at
Schools, Colleges, and Universities

By

WILLIAM G. WILLIAMS

SHARE PUBLISHING COMPANY
P.O. Box 6839, Charlottesville, VA 22906

CONTENTS

PREFACE

Enrollment Strategy contains 102 suggestions for enrollment success at schools, colleges, and universities, plus 16 of the best ideas from *The Enrollment Workbook* (Share Publishing Co., 1978). Each suggestion is accompanied by a brief explanation and is tabulated in a planning check list in Section Sixteen. An attempt has been made to avoid the jargon of marketing, and to express theory in the form of tangible action suggestions.

The 118 suggestions are opinions based on the experience and observations of the author over many years. Not every idea will be appropriate for every institution, and some of the ideas may require modification in order to suit individual circumstances.

It is assumed that readers are committed to enrollment growth, or at least slowed decline, and that they will be willing to take action on many of the suggestions. A possible first step would be to compare each item in the check list with existing policies and practices—resulting in an enrollment strategy score.

THE AUTHOR

William G. Williams earned his Ph.D. in higher education at Florida State University where he was an Education Professions Development Act Fellow. He holds a bachelor's and master's degree from George Washington University. His administrative experience has included posts at Georgetown University, George Washington University, and Piedmont Virginia Community College.

Williams has gained his knowledge of educational marketing from careful study and through many years of experience as a recruiter, financial aid counselor, researcher, and division head. His knowledge is first-hand and practical. He has helped recruit thousands of students, has hired hundreds of instructors, and designed scores of promotional campaigns in a variety of settings—from community college to university, from professional school to adult education—both public and private. He also is a keen observer of other educators, carefully analyzing their enrollment successes and failures.

Williams achieved a tripling of enrollment in his division at Piedmont Virginia Community College between 1974 and 1979 before becoming a full-time writer and consultant specializing in educational marketing and conference management.

The author's publications include articles in the *American Vocational Journal, College and University Business, NASPA Journal, Community College Review, Community College Frontiers,* and other journals, in addition to three books.

7

SECTION ONE

ADMINISTRATIVE COMMITMENT

1. Rate each administrative activity according to its enrollment growth potential.

If an institution is to achieve enrollment growth its leaders must have more than simply a desire for growth. They must make way for growth. This means clearing out numerous administrative distractions which have no enrollment growth potential, and then identifying and giving emphasis to those which do.

For example, a project to revise job descriptions, or to establish a personnel grievance procedure does not have great enrollment growth potential compared with establishment of new courses or extension locations. The effort put into most federal grants and professional activities will not have the enrollment yield of similar attention given to establishing daycare centers, studying community attitudes, or revising mailing lists.

The goal is to focus the administrative process and structure on enrollment growth, because enrollment success is not an accident. Presidents, deans, directors, and others give far too much attention to activities which do not result in healthy enrollments. Often after each disappointing registration there is a period of wringing hands, of pointing fingers—but no real commitment to solving the problem.

2. Establish a clear sense of mission and market position.

Professional staff members at a school, college, or university must be in accord concerning the institution's special ability, emphasis, and personality. All publicity and priorities are then focused on the institution's role and attractions.

For example, a college in Ohio is known for its intellectual, liberal, activist students and faculty, while a state university in the mountains of North Carolina emphasizes its rural, folk culture, developmental studies character in serving mostly first-generation higher education students. A university in Washington, D.C. focuses on a Catholic philosophy together with excellence in liberal arts, government, international affairs, medicine and law. A community college in Maryland provides a huge variety of beginners' courses and is portrayed as an educational shopping center.

Marketing position refers to an institution's establishment of identity, both internally and externally, and the achievement of a favorable position in the minds of its publics—students, prospective students, trustees, faculty, donors, and advisors of students such as high school counselors, employers, and employment agencies.

Educators must not seek increased enrollment in ways which will greatly obscure or confuse their identity or position. For example, educators at the state university already at or near the top of institutions concentrating on folk culture and remedial studies would not be wise to try to shift their image to that of an intellectual center.

3. Keep records of the amount of time devoted to enrollment producing activities.

Most day-to-day activities of administrators do not produce enrollment. These activities include personnel supervision, budget planning, report writing, traveling, committee work, and protecting one's own corner of the campus. Keeping records will help prove that enrollment disappointments result from lack of effort, even among concerned administrators.

Enrollment, after all, is a vote. It is a vote of confidence from students stating that the institution is well regarded, its faculty teaches well, topics are of interest, class locations and times are convenient, fees are appropriate to benefits, etc. One must campaign for enrollment votes, and nearly every effort in the campaign will also serve idealistic educational goals.

4. Make expenditure decisions on the basis of how much enrollment revenue each dollar will return.

A decision, for example, between replacing a pickup truck and hiring six adjunct instructors is obviously one which would result in enrollment growth if the old truck were retained. Adding an accounts payable clerk and a grounds-keeper is not as enrollment productive as hiring an additional admissions recruiter or a person to develop a new extension location.

5. Give revenue producers greater influence over institutional policy than is held by revenue-dependent personnel.

Just as institutional leaders wishing enrollment growth must shift their attention to activities which generate enroll-ment, so too must they place additional decision-making authority in the hands of those who generate enrollment revenue.

For example, the business division chairman at a typical community college has tremendous potential for enrollment growth, but will typically have far less influence over institu-tional direction and priorities than the college business officer. The latter is a person who spends money; the former is a person who earns money. In commerce, earners rule spenders!

A continuing education dean is in a pivotal position to make or break the institution through enrollment success or failure. When compared with the assistant to the president or director of institutional studies, however, most continuing education deans are far outside the administrative mainstream and have little influence over major institutional policies.

If institutional resources and institutional activities are to be those which are invested to generate enrollment revenue, then those investments must be made by revenue builders— not "overhead" personnel.

6. Make decisions regarding buildings and grounds on the basis of enrollment return.

A new parking lot may have a more immediate positive impact on enrollment than the green lawn it replaces. The campus theater, which is used only two or three times each week, might better serve enrollment growth if it were partitioned into classrooms for evening students. Perhaps the lawn and the theater are very important attractions and should be saved. The greater likelihood is that no one has given much thought to these and similar questions regarding enrollment benefit from institutional resources.

7. Appoint an enrollment committee and/or enrollment coordinator.

Most successful towns, cities, counties, and states have development committees or coordinators whose job it is to attract new revenue, new taxpayers, new employment, and new investment.

High priority is given at most institutions of higher education to a development office which generates contributions and prepares grant proposals. However, there is seldom a similar headquarters for revenue attainment through enrollment strategy. Enrollment policy is often divided as part-time jobs of several administrators. A bit is found in admissions, a little in public information, deans of schools often are involved, even faculty with small classes or dying programs may devote part of their effort to enlarging enrollments.

A coordinator or a committee can help increase attention to enrollment growth and can help insure that the intent, timing, and magnitude of enrollment growth measures mesh in mutual reinforcement.

8. Do not initiate new fees or inflate fees when increases in services or in participation would better increase revenue.

One college in Maryland with chronic enrollment and revenue problems recently began charging community organizations for the use of college meeting space. While this practice may earn a few dollars, institutional leaders are reducing visitor traffic to the campus and are creating ill will among citizens, regardless of whether they accept or reject the opportunity to pay to use buildings their taxes helped build.

Perhaps educators should pay the citizens a fee for the use of administrative and faculty offices, or for parking space on campus.

Visitors have a chance to become familiar with the institution and its services. They view student exhibits, obtain class schedules, and begin to feel at home. Educators who place a tax on this enormous source of potential enrollment have a mistaken enrollment strategy, or none at all.

Provide more services to more participants. Only when value or demand is created can prices be increased.

Section Two

MANAGEMENT INFORMATION

SECTION 2

9. Determine the number of service area high school graduates, where such persons study in higher education, and the institution's enrollment share.

While this might seem to be common institutional research data, on many campuses it does not exist. The importance of this information is that educators cannot increase service area populations. Only the share of the population attending the institution can be influenced.

How many students graduate from which high schools? How many are going to distant colleges, to nearby competing institutions, or are not seeking further education at all? Is there one public institution just across the state border which is attracting large numbers of local graduates?

Trends are important over several years of data collection. Students from one region, city, or county may be on the decrease at the college, while another identifiable group has found some perceived advantage and is far better represented at the institution. This calls for further study to identify causes.

A service area may be as small as a county, or it may be state-wide, regional, national or international. For the purposes of this kind of data collection, even large colleges and universities can attain a manageable research focus. A private university in Washington, D.C., for example, could gather data from high schools in New Jersey, New York, Pennsylvania, Maryland, Virginia, and the District of Columbia—perhaps using sampling techniques. High schools in California, Oregon, and Wisconsin would not be high priorities for this institution's studies.

16

10. Study prospective students who visit, write for information, apply, or are admitted, but do not enroll.

The selection of a college or university is a series of small decisions in consumer behavior. Most such small decisions are of a negative or elimination type. A prospective student may consider twenty options, but over weeks or months gradually eliminate one option after another until a decision is finally reached.

Contacts with students who have failed to select an institution can reveal the kinds of considerations that caused the student to go elsewhere. Tuition rate, general reputation, field of study strength, sports facilities, financial aid, and other causes can steer the institution to changes which will reduce its likelihood of being a rejected school.

11. Determine why some students select the institution and enroll.

Enrolled students, often referred to as the "yield," should be questioned regarding which institutional attributes or personal preferences resulted in their registration.

That which convinced them might convince others! Was it the reputation of the faculty, the persuasiveness of a recruiter, the financial aid package, tuition rate, local contacts, emphasis on a certain field of study, non-institutional attractions of the location, or an accompanying friend? Institutional leaders must know why students select their schools in order to appeal to similar motivations of others making enrollment decisions.

12. Conduct research on public knowledge and perceptions of the institution.

One of the most important factors in recruiting local part-time and full-time students is the image of the college or university among local citizens. This is especially true in highly-structured service areas surrounding community colleges, regional university campuses, or locally-focused private institutions.

For example, does the citizen perceive the institution to be highly selective when it is not? Is it considered expensive when actually it is not? Do most citizens consider students to be young when most students are actually middle-aged, and frequently older than the faculty?

The findings of such studies serve more than educational curiosity. Incorrect perceptions can harm enrollments. An experienced retailer, for example, may learn of a course on the state commercial code, but not consider enrollment due to fears that the other students would be young and the course content theoretical. A student may stay away from an attractive art course with naive doubts about being good enough.

Corrections of public misconceptions can follow their identification. Obviously, a favorable misconception would not be high on a list of those to be corrected.

13. Study competing institutions to determine their advantages and disadvantages.

Institutional leaders should compare the desirability of services, fees, personnel, and facilities of competing institutions with those of their own school, college or university. Competing institutions may be across the street or across the nation. Students can help identify competing institutions which they considered in their enrollment decisions.

Enrollment strategy can include correction of weaknesses and better publicity of strengths. Selectivity is important, because it would be too great a burden to surpass a competitor in every aspect of appeal to students.

This type of study is well suited to graduate students or part-time research associates.

14. Obtain data on the enrollment success of academic units and personnel.

Enrollment success data is vital if institutional leaders are to reward growth, and provide leadership for unsuccessful personnel and departments. An instructor with small classes may simply have a poor schedule. An academic division with sagging enrollments may need reorganization or redirection.

Productive personnel work hard for their success, and success itself brings increased workloads with the acquisition of larger numbers of teachers and students. There must be rewards.

Rewards and renewal are founded on knowledge—enrollment success data.

15. Obtain management data on trends in enrollment by race, sex, credit hour load, subject area, age, term enrolled, etc.

Any consideration of actions to be taken by an institution to increase its enrollment should include a study of enrolled student characteristics. There may be shifts in subject popularity, declines in credit hour load, or a decrease in a certain age group which would not be noticed except in data summaries.

Problems are not likely to be solved until they are identified.

16. Determine instructional needs and interests by offering courses, rather than through interest surveys.

It is far more valid and less expensive to determine the popularity of courses simply by offering them, rather than by asking citizens if they would attend. The expense of questionnaires and telephone calls is far greater than that of course cancellations.

Questionnaire responses are not usually well thought out, and the responses to a question and to a learning opportunity are not identical. Citizens will often express interest in course titles with which they are familiar, but enroll in the unfamiliar. That is, they will often respond to a title they recognize—something they already know! The existence of a course, publicity about it, and the instructor's reputation will often arouse interest in some persons who might have ignored a course title in a questionnaire.

Another problem with surveys is that they raise the expectation that each person's wish will be granted, which leads to disappointment.

17. Study commercial markets in an effort to identify productive extension sites.

Many institutions attempting to increase enrollments must discover locations for new extension courses or branch campuses. A study of commercial decisions can reduce the effort involved in identifying popular locations.

Bank branches, convenience stores, and fast food outlets are a few of the clues to good locations. Such locations have been favored by business leaders based on populations and traffic patterns, and extension classes should be housed nearby. Locations in high commercial traffic areas not only provide convenience for students, but also offer numerous opportunities for attracting attention with signs, posters, and handouts.

An extension site should never be referred to as a "satellite center," which is confusing education jargon.

18. Use data in management decisions in order to make changes.

This is a reminder to use data in changing the institution. Enrollment increase is not likely to occur without change, and most changes should be based on objective findings. Management information is not for report writing or for the satisfaction of academic curiosity.

Conversely, each research venture should be put to the test of first asking what decisions or changes could be made based on hypothetical results. For example, it is foolish to ask students their opinion of the campus food service unless funds exist for its improvement.

SECTION THREE

PERSONNEL POLICIES

SECTION 3

19. Require all professional personnel to make an enrollment contribution.

Too often a small number of administrators at a school, college or university is charged with the responsibility for enrollment success. The director of admissions, division chairmen, deans of schools within universities, deans of continuing education and a few others frequently are evaluated at least in part on the success of enrollments in their administrative units. When only a few persons are accountable for enrollment success, the majority of administrators have no incentive to cooperate in what must be a college-wide effort.

For example, the coordinator of institutional studies has an important role to play in furnishing valuable information which can be used to generate enrollment revenue. Institutional research personnel on some campuses are further charged with the responsibility for developing an institutional enrollment marketing plan. Similarly, the public information officer is a key person in publicity and promotion which is easily evaluated by the quality of brochures, the number of press releases, advertising successes and other results. Counselors can assist with in-class early registration and special attractions such as career decision weeks. The librarian or learning resources director can initiate a campaign to provide services to local non-students. The business manager can engage in a campaign to assure that institutional funds and facilities are used in such a way as to promote service to citizens and enrollment revenue production.

Only when there is a team effort, and evaluation of each team member based on enrollment growth, is it likely that enrollment problems will be solved.

20. Award larger salaries and larger increases to enrollment productive administrators.

Members of the administrative staff should be rewarded when their efforts result in enrollment growth and especially when their achievements create larger workloads due to more students and more instructors. It seems only common sense that a successful administrator with a large division and demanding service commitments should receive increased compensation. However, a custom exists in education for rewards to be based on graduate education, professional activities, or popularity among colleagues, rather than efforts to increase services and the number of persons served.

When there is disparity in income and academic rank among individuals based on past practices or length of service, there is a temptation to give larger increases to those with the lower earnings or academic rank. And yet, the individual who is productive considers only his or her own increase, and those increases must be based on current effectiveness. Other ways to reward highly paid, high ranking persons with large administrative units would be to provide an administrative assistant or to divide the unit.

21. Award benefits to enrollment productive administrators, such as extra vacation time, better budgets, larger staffs, less committee work, or more travel.

If personnel policies prevent full rank and salary compensation to productive administrators, or if additional benefits are desired, the institution may reward successful administrators with several days more annual leave, some relief from unproductive activities, staff increases, better offices, desirable travel assignments, or reduction of bothersome committee assignments.

Each person on the staff must know that enrollment is a central goal and that its achievement will have a direct payoff. Persons who are high achievers by nature and who would energetically help build the institution without incentives should, nonetheless, be rewarded as a matter of fairness and as an example for others.

22. Award promotions and other benefits to faculty with large classes.

Not to be forgotten in efforts to reward increased enrollment are those faculty whose teaching skill and personal charisma draw large numbers of students to their classes. These persons, too, must be rewarded, with class size considered in the awarding of rank, tenure and salaries. They too, can receive special benefits for travel, excuse from committee work, better offices, and similar recognition.

23. Provide customer relations training for all institutional personnel.

Assuming that most institutional staff members have no retailing experience or training, it is important to offer training in the art of people pleasing. Airlines, car rental agencies, motel chains and other retail establishments provide customer relations training which extends from answering the telephone to business etiquette. This sort of preparation for consumer contact is quite rare among colleges and universities, but must be provided to each staff member who comes in contact with students or prospective students—and this means *all* staff members.

The first person or perhaps the only person a visitor will meet when visiting to obtain a class schedule for the next semester will be the parking lot attendant, a groundskeeper, or secretary. All employees at the institution must know that their first duty is to make a favorable impression on prospective students.

26

Customer relations training might be contracted through professional firms providing such services. Representatives of the telephone company are a good initial training contact inasmuch as telephone callers feel a special anonymity and remoteness which precludes them toward being defensive and easily offended.

24. Other credentials being equal, give priority in employment to persons with retail business experience.

There is perhaps no experience or training which is better suited to all staff members at schools, colleges, and universities than that provided by retail employment. Many applicants for professional and support positions will have had full-time or part-time retail experience.

Those who have served a supervisor whose financial success depends on pleasing customers and making sales have a unique perspective on human relations which can be gained, perhaps, in no other way. They are taught that the customer is not an interruption; they know that the customer is the reason for doing other things such as shelving stock, ordering merchandise, or maintaining records.

25. Conceal internal disputes from the public and the news media.

Internal disputes involving departments, instructors, and administrators must be understood to be normal aspects of group behavior. Exposure of a conflict to outside parties, who do not readily understand the insignificance of such disagreements, can needlessly undermine public confidence.

At a time when sagging enrollments threaten the careers of many educators, there is no justification for public displays of trivial problems. Citizens learning of campus contention rarely take a side or play an influential role in resolving the conflict! Some citizens will rejoice in fanning the flames of controversy once the smoke has been detected.

Public acceptance of the institution is harmed when citizens perceive a group of colleagues apparently having little respect for each other.

26. Subdue personal causes, religion, politics, etc.

A prospective Police Science student might receive excellent advice from a counselor who is a member of a committee charging law enforcement officials with brutality. A rural student might receive superb instruction from a faculty member who is publicly devoted to the annexation of county land for city taxation. However, when personal causes are openly expressed and exhibited, confidence is often undermined and the student may feel alienated.

Political banners, equal rights posters, religious artifacts, and other similar items of office decoration serve only to call attention to personal differences, personal distance. Occasional friends won through such displays or expressions of opinion are far outnumbered by other persons who come to question the fairness and impartiality with which they will be treated.

Section Four

CAMPUS ENVIRONMENT

SECTION 4

27. Provide an obvious reception area for prospective students and other new visitors.

When approaching an unfamiliar campus, visitors must be able to identify one area where they can make their first contact. There must be one desk or one office where they can get directions, learn names, locate classrooms and simply be made to feel welcome and reassured.

"Good morning, how can we help you . . . Admissions is the second door on the right . . . Yes, your car is properly parked."

28. Post direction signs showing the way to counselors, the community services office, and others.

Often when a visitor approaches a campus it is difficult to locate visitor parking. Signs should direct them to it. From the parking lot, signs should show the way one proceeds to commonly visited locations such as the auditorium, board room, gymnasium, and library.

The only sources of increased enrollment are those persons who are unfamiliar with the campus. The faster and more easily strangers become acquainted with the institution, the better.

29. Assign functional names to college buildings which can be understood by non-students.

A person new to the school, college, or university stares up at large buildings and reads names such as Student Union, Smith Hall, and Conrad's Way. Smith Hall may or may not house the school of nursing, Conrad's Way may or may not lead to the physics laboratory, and some conservatives might question their suitability for union membership.

If the names of benefactors or revered colleagues are to adorn buildings, then let there be dual designations such as Royce Administration Building or Taylor Science Center.

It is no longer acceptable to confuse visitors who may be considering enrollment in college classes. The hundreds of tiny barriers erected over years of a seller's market in education must now be removed.

30. Do not isolate administrators from visiting citizens, students and prospective students.

Occasionally during a hectic day's activities college staff members may be dearly pressed to complete an assignment or to meet an obligation rapidly, and are not available to visitors. More often they are simply floundering in a bureaucratic malaise and would receive valuable rejuvenation from a visitor seeking a mentor's advice. And yet, outer office personnel are frequently assigned the duty of insisting on appointments or of providing minimal information with the goal of rerouting a visitor to another office.

Any faculty member, administrator, or counselor who does not welcome unscheduled visits might consider the appropriateness of a career change.

A public impression of heavy work loads and inaccessiblity has considerable ego satisfaction, and there is some career risk in one's seeming to be too unoccupied, but student visits should receive high priority. Office personnel can simply state that they have been instructed to interrupt the dean's busy schedule when citizens or students visit.

31. Do not screen telephone calls, ask the names of callers, or the nature of their calls.

Many educators flatter themselves that they will receive large numbers of demanding telephone calls, and that they are busy meeting mounds of commitments which prevent them from answering the telephone. However, when their secretaries are absent for a day they may be astonished to learn how few calls they actually receive, and what great satisfaction and knowledge their protection has denied them.

Telephone callers know who they are and the nature of their business. They know they are important and believe others should consider them important. To them, stating their name and the nature of their business is superfluous. Repeating it again, from outer office secretary to private secretary, is to them further redundant. When the caller finally reaches the administrator and again must repeat identification and the nature of the call, the caller is annoyed and ready for trouble!

32. Be certain that all buildings, grounds, equipment, and furnishings are orderly, clean, and in good repair.

One college in Virginia often has a food service truck parked on the main student walkway to a classroom building. The truck is ugly and frequently tracks mud onto the walkway. Another institution with an automobile service program has partially disassembled old hulks of cars strewn about one corner of its campus. Broken pencil sharpeners, dirty tables and chairs, dusty halls, lawns of potato chip bags, and parking lots paved with cola cans are common on many campuses.

Campuses become uninvitingly shabby very gradually and those who work or study in messy surroundings each day barely notice the slow deterioration. Visitors will notice. They can see that educators do not care about the campus, and can only wonder if college personnel care about anything.

Section Five

COURSE ANNOUNCEMENTS

SECTION 5

33. Make class schedules simple, brief and uncluttered.

The Spring 1980 course announcement newspaper insert published by a Maryland community college serves as an example of mistakes which should be avoided. (The institution has persistent public acceptance problems.) While the course offerings easily could be listed on four or five pages, the 25-page announcement is cluttered with irrelevant illustrations, self-defeating warnings about travel costs, and chopped-up unrelated notices.

Many of the ingredients are proper, but their mixture and alternating formats are very confusing. There are scores of different styles and sizes of type. Some lines of type are vertical, some horizontal, some at an angle, and some are upside down! Most of what the announcement conveys is chaos.

Start with what the institution has to sell—instruction. Present it boldly and simply. Other details can follow in a pleasant arrangement covering admissions, registration, parking, etc.

The announcement might be field tested by showing drafts to family and friends in order to obtain their reactions and suggestions. See if they can find a particular course such as Consumer Economics. Ask them when and where they would go for registration. Ask them how much money they would be prepared to pay, where they would park, etc. See how long it takes them to find such information. Look for signs of frustration.

No institution with enrollment revenue problems can justify the expense of a 25-page course announcement in which the course list occupies only five pages.

34. Avoid reliance on newspaper insert course announcements.

Newspaper advertisements are an important part of an institution's publicity campaign, but reliance on newspaper tabloid inserts as the major publicity vehicle is an error. All households do not receive newspapers. In suburban areas or small cities surrounding large metropolitan areas, a reader may subscribe to only one of a half dozen newspapers. Further, newspapers contain much information of competing interest—sports, local events, classified ads, business reports, international news, the obituaries, comics, etc. All these compete for the reader's attention and the tabloid class schedule will be ignored in many instances. Mounds of other advertising in the newspaper can also distract the reader.

35. Repeat course publicity in various forms and at various times in order to gain maximum coverage and to achieve reinforcement through repetition.

Publicity for the schedule of classes should include newspaper listings, preferably on the back page of a section or in a weekly television guide. Some classes such as those with prerequisites might be deleted due to space limitations. When there is more than one newspaper serving an area, as many newspapers as possible should be used even if some of the lists are abridged.

A complete schedule can be bulk mailed to households in the institution's service area. The schedule would include all courses and other details such as parking regulations and bookstore hours.

The same type of class schedule as is bulk mailed should be distributed on campus and mailed to former local students and others on record as having contacted the institution for information.

The above steps are in reverse order of timing. The first step is to hand out copies of the schedule in class before the end of preceding term. The bulk mailing, mailing to former students, and mailing to inquirers can take place after the distribution on campus. Newspaper advertisements occur last.

The addition of short radio announcements, talk shows, posters, and targeted mailings will insure maximum coverage and public awareness of the institution's learning opportunities.

36. Publish only one alphabetical sequence of classes in the course schedule and do not categorize classes by time or location.

Readers who open the course schedule announcement and begin to scan a list of classes may not find topics of interest in their proper alphabetical location because the desired classes are taught in the evening and readers were looking at the day class list. Or, readers may look only at the main campus list and not the extension site lists. Even the reader who finds the proper list, for example evening classes at Wilson High School, is being encouraged to ignore courses at all other sites and times. Such a reader may be looking for an Acrylics Painting class in a favorite location, and finding none, may not be willing to look through several other lists for Acrylics at other acceptable times and locations. This is a common, costly, and easily avoidable problem. Educators must not assume that many prospective students will notice several class lists and make the effort to read them.

If the institution offers no Acrylics Painting courses, but all the art classes are together in one list, the reader may discover other art classes of interest such as Stained Glass Art, and Ceramics.

Using a properly designed single list, any person limited strictly to a certain time, day, or location can easily self-select for these variables.

37. Provide an alphabetical index of classes if departmental or other groupings make classes difficult to find.

If Art is listed under Humanities, if Solar Energy is listed under Environmental Science, and if Real Estate is listed under Marketing—then there must be an alphabetical index to courses.

Of course, it is wiser to eliminate arbitrary groupings which only obscure the availability of classes, but the index will reduce the seriousness of the problem.

38. Avoid confusing abbreviations.

Publicity is for the uninformed. The greater the requirements or expectations of prior knowledge, the less effective is the promotional effort.

"M-W" means the class meets three days per week, or two? "2 Hr Lab/TBA" means there will be about twice as much work required as for other three-credit classes and the lab time is to be announced—or arranged? Now, what does "Per Inst" mean?

39. Publish pictures and biographies of counselors and other public contact personnel.

A successful manufacturer of precision tools pictures three persons on the first page of its catalog with a name and a telephone number below each. Readers are invited to telephone the first of the three employees in order to discuss tool design and materials, the second to place an order, and the third to obtain information on billings and shipping. A leading yacht broker in Florida publishes pictures and the interests of its sales staff in boating magazines. One agent is primarily interested in sport fishing, another in power cruising, another in sailboat racing, etc.

These money-making firms take pains to establish personal identities which lead to customer compatibility and reduce the need to reroute telephone calls or correspondence. A person wishing a special tool design will be more likely to approach the manufacturer if the name and face of the design engineer are known. A power boat cruising enthusiast will be encouraged to contact the yacht broker if there is an agent particularly interested in power cruising.

If prospective students are made familiar with the ages, interests, backgrounds, and other characterisitcs of counselors, admissions personnel, and others, client-preselection of an appropriate staff member can occur. This is a valuable first step, a step which might never be taken without the biographical information. Senior citizens might prefer to speak with an older counselor, veterans may wish to contact another veteran, while the needs of a woman head-of-household might be best understood by a college staff member in similar circumstances.

SECTION SIX

PUBLIC AWARENESS BUILDERS

SECTION 6

40. Display exhibits of student learning in order to stimulate course interest.

It is not unusual for art or crafts students to have a show, or even a sale, each term. Students of drama or music have productions which display their achievements and inspire similar goals in others.

Displays by students in other subject areas would also help build pride of achievement and stimulate enrollment interest in specific fields. Students of solar energy could build a working solar collection unit and display it near a building entrance. Each component of the collector could be labeled, and its function described. Investment students could display records of stocks, real estate, metals, jewels, and other investments. Data processing students could take some of their fascinating equipment out of the laboratory and show others the role of printers, sorters, computers, etc. Students of vegetarian cookery could prepare small hand-out quantities of their meatless meals.

41. Use a focus board or enlarged type size to call attention to enrollment-building classes.

Existing students know how to locate listings for the second semester of English Composition or the third quarter of Chemistry. These and similar course listings can be squeezed among the many crowded lines of type in a typical course announcement, but should not be eliminated. The common practice of eliminating sequential courses from some copies of the class schedule is an error. No course should be eliminated, except from abbreviated newspaper advertisements, if the loss of one student might result.

Growth during the year will depend on new study entry opportunities such as one-term electives or special interest courses. Entry opportunities should be printed in extra large type and/or be featured on focus boards.

A focus board is prepared by placing each side of each page of the class listings in sequence on a large bulletin board—perhaps ten feet wide and six feet high. Around the abundant margins of the course listings large labels are pinned up showing the names of such courses as Nutrition, Real Estate, Personal Typing, Song Writing, or Consumer Car Care. The labels should be approximately two by four inches in size with large letters. A thin strip of colored paper or yarn leads from each large course label to its relatively obscure course listing on the pages of the schedule.

Course descriptions are no substitute for type enlargements or focus boards. Course descriptions clutter a schedule and occupy too much of a reader's time.

42. Provide recorded telephone messages on courses, programs, and registration details.

Recorded telephone messages are recommended which provide basic consumer information on the institution and the ways to benefit from its services. Many persons are overwhelmed by course publicity. Others are initially timid about conversations or implied commitments resulting from personal contact. Both groups may respond to recorded capsules of information concerning registration, study requirements, student profiles, times, and dates.

The anonymity of calling 338-6512 as a first step is extremely important for many persons. The recorded message should be reassuring and introductory.

Availability of the recorded telephone information can be publicized in small newspaper advertisements and brief radio announcements. All brochures, catalogs, and other institutional information might also list the service.

43. Insure that all public announcements and correspondence support enrollment goals.

Institutions of higher education produce numerous public announcements and voluminous correspondence which can contain enrollment messages. For example, help wanted advertisements are perhaps the best read section of newspapers and can include enrollment promotion. An advertisement for the employment of clerical or groundskeeping personnel can mention registration dates, specific courses, or the institution's placement service.

Other locations for enrollment messages are athletic programs, concert programs, invoices, purchase orders, envelopes, and envelope inserts. A business college in Oregon includes a printed description of its services, facilities, and staff in all correspondence. The insert's 20 by 9 inch size provides much information, yet the thin sheet folds to a convenient and light-weight letter envelope size.

Information on accounting classes, data processing, and other business related topics is especially appropriate to accompany accounts payable and accounts receivable correspondence. Similarly, information on music, art and athletics courses can receive specialized placement.

44. Identify professional personnel in order to invite inquiries concerning the institution.

Real estate agencies commonly identify their sales staff by means of pins, blazers, or other devices, while educational institutions usually only identify their janitorial staff and athletes. Teachers and counselors will almost always wear a name and institution tag at professional meetings, but never at neighborhood meetings.

Family members and friends often turn to educators for information and advice on careers, training, investments, or even basketball tickets. Administrators at a growing institution will encourage a proliferation of such contacts by making their professional personnel identifiable to strangers. A stranger is more likely to be among the unserved citizens than a professor's neighbor or relative, and is therefore a more likely prospect for enrollment growth.

45. Provide college plaques for the offices of successful part-time instructors.

At many institutions which respond to a broad range of specialized student learning interests, the number of adjunct faculty members may reach or exceed that of the full-time faculty. Most adjuncts are leaders in their fields of endeavor and in community service. Attorneys, bankers, manufacturers, real estate brokers, engineers, journalists, broadcasters, government officials, and retailers are examples.

Each such teacher/leader enjoys many relationships of trust and respect in the community, and a school plaque proudly displayed in the adjunct's office will bring recognition to both the instructor and the institution. A plaque will often turn conversations to the school, college or university. When asked, part-time instructors will likely promote their own classes and recommend the institution generally.

The plaque might be made an award for one, two, or more years of service.

46. Provide signs to personnel offices in recognition of training projects.

Many personnel offices of firms in the institution's community should be under contract for in-service training projects or tuition support for their employees. A sign in the personnel office will call attention to the acceptance of the institution by the firm, and will also remind the many seekers of employment of the relationship between education and employment.

The public information officer should be certain to include the school, college, or university in grand-opening announcements of new firms to which training or trained personnel have been provided.

47. Distribute institutional reminders such as catalogs, class schedules, conference folders, and calendars to visitors and other citizens.

A major purpose of community services and other campus visitor attractions is to benefit the many non-students who helped build the institution and pay salaries through direct tax support or institutional tax exemptions. Once citizens are on campus for special events, an opportunity exists to distribute class schedules, catalogs, curricular program announcements, and other reminders that the institution offers additional opportunities for entertainment, self-improvement, and community development.

Such reminders taken home or to the office are often kept for many days or weeks and serve to keep the institution's message at hand for repeated reference. Fond memories of a drama production or town meeting are of great benefit, but a broader and more tangible awareness of opportunities provided by the school, college, or university must be sought.

48. Give recognition to sponsors of special events.

Sponsors of special events at the school, college, or university include many prestigious persons, organizations, and agencies. Avocational clubs, charitable organizations, political parties, service clubs, area governments, and trade groups sponsor meetings, hearings, displays and other activities on most campuses.

Educators should seek to identify their institutions with such sponsors by publishing news releases, a monthly schedule of events, and an annual summary of special activities listing each sponsor. These notices will have the effect of demonstrating mutual acceptance by the institution and the activity sponsors. A college certificate of appreciation or plaque can be awarded to each sponsor with the hope that it will be displayed in the sponsor's office. The plaque or certificate could have the institution's seal or logo in the center, with the words "In Appreciation" across the top, and "Special Events Sponsor" at the bottom.

Special events sponsors should be asked if there is any instruction the institution could offer which would further the cause of the sponsor. The special activity might itself be of an instructional nature, such as a one-day demonstration of print making or stone setting. Hopefully, sponsors and participants will be retained as teachers and students in related classes to follow.

SECTION SEVEN

STUDENT SERVICES

SECTION 7

49. Offer a wide range of student activities for the pursuit of special interests and the development of leadership skills.

Local students will often forsake a nearby institution which does not offer sufficient co-curricular opportunities related to student interests such as in journalism, student government, broadcasting, drama, and chorus. Such students may seek enrollment at other larger and perhaps distant institutions with great expectations of becoming members of an active campus choir, large student newspaper, student court, or busy theater group.

Educators should study popular student activities at high schools in their service areas in order to anticipate the activity interests of prospective students, and to provide a higher education followup for the continuing expression of interests and the development of skills. Subject area clubs such as those for students of business, agriculture, foreign languages, art, music, and dance should also be sponsored and will be attractive to many potential students.

Meager student activity offerings are especially common at community colleges, and community college educators often report a lack of student interest. "Students just come here for classes and then they disappear," it is often said. One might question whether students avoid activities on some campuses, or if students avoid campuses without activities.

After years of limited activities it is not likely that immediate or spontaneous activity renewal will occur. There must be sustained institutional cultivation, and perhaps a disproportionate contribution in college staff time and institutional funding before an activity campaign will become sustained by students.

While activities are in a renewal phase there are increased opportunities for student impact and leadership, which has recruitment advantages. For example, prospective students can be offered an opportunity to help found and manage a student radio station, rather than merely try out for an announcing position at an established station of another institution.

50. Award student leaders grants in support of student activities.

Many institutions of postsecondary education should increase financial aid to student activity leaders. Such awards can greatly increase awareness of the institution among influential high school students, will attract able students who might fall slightly below requirements for academic scholarships, and will enhance student life on campus. Academic scholarship holders often contribute nothing to the institution or to the college experience of other students.

Activity awards can be made to editors of the student newspaper, officers in student government, band members, and many others in a variety of patterns suitable for differing institutions. Financial need criteria can commonly be avoided by offering tuition waivers or college-paid hourly employment when such support is not funded by means of reductions in need-based financial aid.

51. Promote activities for part-time students.

Many part-time students who enroll in classes are likely to disengage from study after one quarter or semester. They commonly sense a lack of belonging. If they become a part of the institution at all it is limited to one class which inevitably ends—ending their involvement.

49

Part-time students should be encouraged to have their own newspaper and their own section of the student center, to become involved with student government and with clubs and organizations. Many part-time students are as much interested in fellowship as in learning. They often feel that full-time students have a monopoly on camaraderie and student identity.

At mostly residential institutions there should also be special student services for full-time commuting students.

52. Assist youth groups in the attainment of their goals.

Popular associations for young persons such as Scouts, 4-H, Junior Achievement, and high school clubs can be served in many ways by educators at postsecondary educational institutions. Scouts may simply need a few acres on which to pitch their tents. A 4-H club may need a large auditorium for its public speaking contests. Junior Achievement could be advised by the business administration faculty or students, and many high school clubs could be invited to enter into big brother or big sister agreements.

Each young person who becomes familiar with a nearby collegiate institution can be expected at least to consider that institution in a later college enrollment decision. Friends and families of college-involved young persons may experience a secondary sense of goodwill.

53. Encourage prestige transfer.

Prestige transfer occurs when a student who enrolls in a sound, perhaps local, college or university with limited national reputation later transfers and graduates from a more prestigious institution, rather than studying all four years at a middle-reputation, compromise school. One student's compromise college is another's first choice, so prestige transfer is an individual, relative decision. Students following well-designed prestige transfer plans can enhance their future opportunities in employment and graduate study.

Prestige transfer might be a formal program, a counseling emphasis, or an occasional suggestion to students. As a recruiting tool it can enable some of the more obscure institutions to sell themselves as a potential package with other better known schools. The plan can have financial benefits to educators who can concentrate on less costly lower division courses. Students and their families can reduce expenses if the initial institution is of low cost or near home.

Transfer is not wise for every student. It is not suitable for some college curricula and some student circumstances. However, large numbers of students have transfer intentions or options in mind, and enrollment builders cannot ignore realities or possibilities.

54. Hold an annual reception or party for the families of enrolled students.

Schools, colleges, and universities often have a special night or open house campus visit for the families of prospective, rather than enrolled, students. The families of existing students who pay the bills, forgo employment income, help type reports, miss out on full-time family activities, and maintain quiet study hours, are often taken for granted. Loyalty to an enrolled student's mother, father, spouse, brother, sister, or friends is well deserved, and each is a potentially important, credible recruiter. Members of a prospective student's family, by contrast, may perceive themselves as part of an institution's self-serving sales campaign.

Once the families of enrolled students are on campus, they should be allowed to be the focus of attention, rather than be a captive audience for some local politician or dean. Students or parents should make speeches. They might share common experiences in group discussions. Entertainment, exhibits, meals and other tangibles in the program should support, not distract from, the intangible to be sought—belonging.

51

55. Provide convenient, responsive channels for student complaints and suggestions.

If students are disappointed with instruction, housing, food services, or counseling, they should have administrative outlets for the expression of their concerns. Weeks or months of frustration over problems can result in a contamination of public and student attitudes toward the institution. Not every complaint is valid, but each is worthy of investigation. Repeated complaints deserve action.

A complaining student will feel an immediate need for communication. The student will become further antagonized if the complaint is not at least recognized, or worse, leads to no solution. A student opinion hour with the college president or dean provides spontaneous recognition. Action or explanation is required for all complaints or comments.

Two examples of complaint reactions may add perspective. Students at one college complained of library noise, so a quiet reading room was partitioned within the existing library area. By contrast, students at the same institution argued for an improved food service, and the college's board hired an independent caterer for its own luncheon meetings on campus.

CLASS SCHEDULING

SECTION 8

56. Rotate the time, day, and location of special interest courses each term.

It is a great scheduling convenience to always offer Stained Glass Art, Personal Typing, Home Repair, Consumer Economics, Weaving, Creative Writing, or Spanish Conversation on the same evenings and in the same rooms each term. In this way the instructors have a consistent schedule, the rooms are reserved and administrative planning efforts are few.

However, if special interest courses are to achieve their enrollment growth potential, they must appeal to new students each term. When such courses are scheduled for varying times, days, and locations each term they come into proper phase with the weekly commitments of more and more potential students.

Many traditional evening classes would occasionally succeed at a daytime hour. A course commonly offered off campus on Tuesdays, should be moved on campus on Thursdays. There are many other possibilities.

57. Investigate career certification and licensing requirements in order to offer appropriate training.

There is a strong trend in state governments to increase educational requirements for initial career licensing and renewal. Such requirements apply to nursing, real estate, teaching, insurance, private investigation, pest control and many other careers. Examples of courses in just one occupational field are Real Estate Sales, Real Estate Investments, Real Estate Appraisal, Real Estate Law, Real Estate Financing, and Property Management.

Administrators should prepare a list of all educational requirements in their states and offer those courses suited to the institution's mission. State legislators will often know of new requirements under consideration.

There are additional national requirements for training such as those of the Federal Aviation Administration, FAA. Any school, college, or university can offer the classroom portion of aviation requirements such as Pilots Ground School, Instrument Ground School, and Aviation Regulations, when taught by an FFA-certified instructor. There are also professional society training requirements, and instructional opportunities for test preparation.

No course is so attractive as a required course, especially when the institution does not make the requirement. Instruction required by law or for other certification is well suited to extension sites in population centers distant from the main campus.

58. Do not cancel small classes of eight or more students.

Many institutions with enrollment revenue problems are quick to cancel small classes with the rationale that a certain average class size must be attained in order to achieve a desired financial equilibrium. It is not unusual for a school, college or university to cancel several dozen small classes each term.

A student in a canceled class who visits the campus once to register, a second time for the first class meeting, and perhaps a third time to discover whether or not enough new students have been added, will not soon forget the bad experience. A wait of six to ten weeks for a refund will further build hostility.

Students in canceled classes will eagerly tell friends of their misfortune. It can become common knowledge in an institution's service area that registration is only a poor gamble, and many citizens will begin to ignore course announcements and publicity. Thus, the financial equilibrium desired by administrators becomes increasingly unattainable.

59. Avoid image-destroying courses.

Local tastes and expectations vary widely, so institutional leaders should be aware of public attitudes in their service areas concerning the proper role of a school, college, or university. Certain courses, such as Belly Dancing or Disco Dancing, may be tempting offerings for educators seeking enrollment growth, but such classes are really more appropriate to recreation departments.

A course which serves twenty eager students, but which destroys the image of the college in the minds of several thousand citizens, will not help to build long-term enrollment growth.

Prospective full-time students and their parents are especially sensitive to the professional bearing of an institution. Jokes about certain colleges and universities offering majors in basket weaving are common. Perception is reality, and obvious frivolity must be avoided.

60. Offer numerous educational opportunities on weekends.

Many institutions which lack adequate classroom space are forced to offer classes on weekends and Friday nights. At other colleges and universities there may be under-used classroom space, with the result that educators may not have discovered that there are large numbers of persons who prefer weekend classes due to career and family commitments during the week.

Saturday morning classes should be of a special interest variety such as Art, Photography, The American Short Story, or Song Writing, and not merely be the second or third weekly meeting of Biology or Economics. Sunday afternoon classes are especially successful when they are of a philosophical, historical, or intellectual nature, such as the Life and Times of a local historical figure. Friday night classes also warrant an attempt.

For an institution to have a successful enrollment strategy its class schedule must be in phase with the weekly schedules of as many prospective students as is possible.

61. Ask students in class which course topics interest them for subsequent semesters or quarters.

A suggestion in *The Enrollment Workbook* was to take time out from class meetings to inform students of related courses to be offered in the next academic term. It may be even more productive to ask students to *suggest* courses for addition to the class schedule of the next or later terms. Students in Introduction to Solar Energy may wish a follow-up course on the tangible aspects of solar system installations such as plumbing and electrical details. Students in Pesticide Management or Horse Management may have otherwise unexpressed interests in courses dealing with small farm financial management or farm taxation.

Students can be asked if they would actually enroll in the courses they recommend, and their names and telephone numbers could be collected for use in notification. Preferred days, times, and locations could also be learned.

Registered students are far better prospects for later enrollment than are members of the general public, despite the more common involvement of non-students in learning interest surveys.

62. Analyze the class schedule each term prior to its publication in order to insure sufficient enrollment capacity.

One of the most important considerations in the formulation of a course schedule for a growing institution is to insure that the variety of topics, the number of sections, the number of locations, the number of special interest sponsors, and the amount of assignment rotation will result in successful enrollment. The proposed schedule from each division should be tentatively assigned a number of expected students, and only after all the numbers add up to growth is schedule planning ended and schedule production begun.

It is best to anticipate declines in average class size and in average credit hour load, thus increasing the likelihood that surprises will be favorable.

63. Corroborate employer advice on new courses and programs.

Some unsuccessful new courses or curricula are added to institutional offerings based on poor advice from employers. A small percentage of employers do not understand the investment made in educational offerings or the commitment educators feel toward the employment success of students. An employer may express a need for thirty electronics technicians, for example, when the real desire is for thirty applicants to fill two jobs. A personnel office manager may have one or two very troublesome vacancies and state that the firm is "just dying to get applicants." Needs for trained employees must be carefully distinguished from desires to build applicant pools, and isolated employer frustrations.

Confirmation of trained employee needs can be obtained through other employers, state employment commissions, high school counselors, help wanted advertisements, and private employment agencies. Prospective employers might be asked if they would help plan or pay partial expenses for new offerings.

Occasionally the training requested by employers is for a position classification which is highly undesirable and involves large resignation rates. Enrollment success is not easily built upon preparation for jobs which lead to dissatisfaction.

64. Give attention to forecasting or futurism in order to take advantage of learning interests concerning changes in government, natural resources, economics, demographics, and culture.

If an institution is to grow and serve its students well its leaders must be looking forward in anticipation of new instructional opportunities. Only in this way will the institution be prepared to benefit from new learning interests, and be able to prepare its students for successful lives and careers.

Some examples of futuristic topics are alternative fuels, land use, self-sufficiency, and conservation. From the field of futurism come enticing course titles or course segments such as anticipatory democracy, peace studies, discontinuity, holistics, appropriate technology, and post-affluence.

A Futurism course itself is a promising idea and several universities offer curricula in the field (the University of Massachusetts, University of Hawaii, Fairleigh Dickinson, and others). The U.S. Congress and several state governments have futures agencies, and there are growing numbers of futures societies, publications, and consulting firms.

Private institutions should take advantage of their ability to respond quickly to change. Most public institutions of higher education are increasingly rule-bound by state coordinating agencies.

SECTION NINE

RECRUITMENT IDEAS

SECTION 9

65. Inform adjunct faculty members that part of their assignment is to promote their courses.

Many part-time instructors, especially those new to teaching, do not realize that they can help promote their courses. Part-timers are often disappointed when their classes are canceled due to low enrollments, and express frustration that they were not adivsed to help in achieving enrollment success.

Part-time instructors should be told that part of their preparation is to mention their classes to colleagues, clients, customers, and friends. They can also assist in the production of posters, news releases, and other publicity such as radio and television talk shows. They should be informed that they can help administrators, if not push administrators, in the required promotional efforts.

Attorneys, business persons, and others who obtain public visibility advantages from their part-time teaching will attain additional benefits from their involvement in course publicity.

66. Sponsor a regional job and educational opportunity fair.

A job and educational opportunity fair is a one- or two-day event on campus which enables employers, educational institutions, and members of the public to share information on needs, services, and opportunities regarding careers and training for careers. High school educators must be involved in order to arrange class time visits of eleventh and twelfth grade students. Educators and employers set up booths which often include equipment such as computers for which trained personnel are sought. The sponsoring institution invites its competitors, and the recruitment of students and employees is understood by all to take place.

The value of the fair as an enrollment builder is that large numbers of career decision makers will attend, and that much of the information provided will be in the nature of selection and referral. Well-informed decision making and referral help all participants. Sources of information are concentrated in one location and there is great efficiency of time and effort.

By being able to involve important employers and other educators, the sponsoring institution gains the stature of being a center for career and educational planning.

67. Place college and university information at tourist centers.

When families are on vacations, short weekend trips, or family visits, they are almost always traveling to a location which holds for them one or more important attractions. The area visited could have a desirable climate, recreational activities, or cultural opportunities. The area could be the home of relatives or friends the travelers wish they could see more often. The trip could be a return to an earlier place of residence. In any case, the travelers should have an opportunity to learn of the educational opportunities provided by local educational institutions seeking enrollment growth.

College brochures should be placed in the racks of tourist information centers and motel lobbies. College information should appear in printed tourist guides, or "This Week in Smithville" booklets which are often available at restaurants, places of lodging, and tourist centers. The campus might even be listed among the significant places to visit—it should be on all maps.

When prospective students make their selections of colleges or universities at which to spend several years of study, vacation sites and campuses they have visited under holiday circumstances will receive better than average consideration.

68. Establish a campus travelers attraction or tourist information center.

In many cases the college or university itself is a potential tourist attraction. Many educators overlook the opportunity to draw travelers to their site by means of a regional museum, significant art exhibit, planetarium, music festival, or other attraction. Actually obtaining a family's presence on campus will yield a far more positive influence than mere printed information.

A college information booth near the campus museum or drama production can distribute printed material and answer questions regarding the school. College mementos might be sold.

On the author's campus a large Bicentennial Center was built in 1976 through a grant of college land. For a year or more a one-hour drama production on the life and times of Thomas Jefferson was staged in the college auditorium based on invitations to the many visitors of the Bicentennial Center. This was a special opportunity for one institution. Each has its own.

69. Offer campus activities for local students visiting home from distant institutions.

Many high school students planning their higher educations at distant colleges or universities have fond illusions which are not fulfilled once the student actually enrolls and attends for one or more academic terms.

When students return home for winter or spring vacations, opportunities should be available for these absentee students to realize that there are desirable alternatives for education in their own home towns. Vacation time attractions might include athletic events, concerts, or perhaps class reunion activities. There could be a New Year's party or folk festival.

Presenting options to those who have decided to transfer is a legitimate activity for an institution seeking enrollment growth.

70. Invite local prospective students to attend visitors class sessions.

Instructors should be encouraged to make available visitors nights or bring-a-friend sessions which would acquaint potential full-time and part-time students with some of the institution's best instruction each term. The visitors might be friends of students or other citizens invited from the community. Instructors could receive help in selecting the most appropriate lessons and in modifying them to suit both the regular students and the visitors. Publicity would direct inquiries to a coordinator who would schedule visits, assist instructors, and furnish information to visitors.

Large numbers of citizens drive past a campus each day, read class schedules each term, and listen to radio and television announcements for years without enrolling. An invitation from a friend or from the institution to attend a visitors class can help break down the barriers of hesitation.

71. Videotape counselors and others as they conduct admissions interviews.

Counselors and others who discuss enrollment with prospective students should be videotaped, and most institutions have equipment readily available. The recorded interviews might best be role-playing sessions involving two or more institutional representatives. Such interviews will help reveal strengths and weaknesses in the interview procedures, can confirm the validity of information provided, can assist beginners to anticipate unfamiliar questions, and can help representatives share successful techniques.

65

Faculty members and administrators should also be encouraged to participate. Exchanges with prospective students could be broadened to include enrolled students and a wide range of subjects such as academic probation, discipline, grade appeals, and student-employee training.

It is important for educators to see themselves as others see them, especially at an institution seeking enrollment success.

72. Encourage counselors and advisors to refer students and prospective students to colleagues.

Referral in counseling, advising, and admissions is very important. Often the initial pairing of a student or potential student with a college representative will be made on an accidental basis depending on who is on duty at a certain time, who answers the telephone, an alphabetical coincidence, or even a data processing error.

Once the counselee and the institutional representative have had an opportunity to become acquainted, it may be obvious that another professional at the institution could better advise the student and build a more successful mentor relationship. When educational clients perceive that they are in the wrong office they may reject the entire institution. A student or prospective student cannot know all the other professionals, their personalities, and their special areas of interest and knowledge.

The initial college representative can make very wise and well-informed referral suggestions leading to enrollment or to retention.

73. Invite families and friends of prospective students to admissions interviews when there is to be a shared decision.

Many persons who visit an admissions office or a college counselor will express a need to discuss their enrollment decision with parents, a spouse, friends, employers, or others. Such prospective students may truly need advice and reassurance, or they may have decided not to enroll and use the advice dodge as a polite way to end the interview. In either case, it is wise to suggest that students bring their advisors to subsequent meetings. Disinterested persons will not return, and those who do return will benefit from sharing their decision with both the college representative and their personal advisors.

Personal advisors should be involved in discussions because most are not well informed on the merits of various institutions, or on educational planning. Comparative costs and benefits among several institutions, financial aid, transfer policies, appropriateness of goals, and other concerns of advisors should be discussed with the prospective student and the institutional representative. Only in this way can educators protect themselves and students from the errors of personal advisors.

Furthermore, the institution might enroll the advisor or the advisor's other friends in addition to the original prospect.

74. Allow prospective students to enroll at the time of admissions interviews or pre-enrollment counseling.

Although commercial comparisons may seem out of place to some educators, it is unusual for customers to approach a business firm and be allowed only to discuss merchandise or services, and not to buy. A typical restaurateur does not discuss meals with patrons and then insist that they return in three weeks in order to dine. Electrical appliance dealers are certainly available to describe and demonstrate their products even if the customer is not ready to buy, but if a sale can be made, it will be made without delay. In the professional realm, it is common for most physicians and dentists to begin diagnosis and treatment on the first visit.

Admissions personnel and counselors should be able to enroll students at any time prior to the beginning of classes, and not insist that students return to wait in line on some distant Tuesday. The institution may have a policy of providing students with an opportunity to ponder their enrollment decisions. However, delays between admissions interviews and registration are almost always a bureaucratic convenience for administrators rather than a professional consideration of a student's best interests.

Educators seeking enrollment growth must not prevent students from enrolling.

SECTION TEN

REGISTRATION

SECTION 10

75. Make student parking spaces available to visitors during registration, as well as meals and other conveniences.

Many persons actually enjoy shopping trips, even when they plan no purchases, but are simply investigating various products. Shopping can be a pleasurable outing—fun! Friends are often invited along, and a delicious lunch may be the highlight of the day. By contrast, registration for instruction is a loathsome obligation, a necessary ordeal to be endured—and often *avoided*.

When a person considers registration, one of the first concerns will be parking. They may have no parking sticker or their parking permit may have expired. This one small barrier may negatively influence a significant number of prospective students. Signs and other publicity should make it clear that student parking areas will be open during registration. Hoods can be placed over parking restriction signs and parking meters.

Also, the food service, library, bookstore, and counseling center should be available. Music, art exhibits and other forms of entertainment might be featured as special attractions, or to soothe the pains of standing, waiting, asking, following, replanning, and paying at registration.

76. Insure that at least one half of the teaching faculty is on campus during all times of registration.

Registration should not be a vacation time for educators, especially those interested in enrollment success. Professional meetings, family travel, and other off-campus activities must be assigned low priority during registration, which is the time when students vote their confidence in the institution with their dollars. Registration is a harvest, the happiest and most rewarding days of the year. What educator would want to miss this period of confirmation when students cast their votes of confidence in months of institutional planning and years of teaching excellence?

Too often during registration only the cashier's office is fully represented. Students have important questions concerning course content, books, assignments, prerequisites, curricular planning, course waivers, and other matters the faculty can best answer. Deans and directors must also plan to be available to the educational customers, and not "in meetings," long lunches, or tied down with appointments which could easily be scheduled before or after registration. Part-time instructors should expect to receive telephone calls at their homes and offices during registration.

Why are representatives of political candidates always at voting precinct locations on election day?

77. Inform all registration workers immediately of canceled classes, filled classes, and especially new classes and sections.

Registration is typically conducted in long hallways, through a series of classrooms, or in large gymnasiums. As a student travels from one registration station to another, the class that was in the student's schedule at station A may have no space available when the student finally arrives at station H. In many cases the communications problem cannot be avoided, as time and many persons pass through the registration procedure. It is quite common, however, for hours and even days of delay to occur before notification reaches all stations that a certain class has been canceled, filled, or added.

An alert division chairperson may add a new section of a popular course, only to find that students are sent away because of lack of information. When the newly available class is fully recognized, perhaps one half of the potential enrollment will have been lost. Thus, there may be twelve students in a class which might have enrolled twenty or more.

The disappointment of a person turned away from a class which was really open is a minor problem when compared with the hostility generated when the rejected person learns three weeks later that a friend registered in the new section on the same day it was reported to be unavailable.

78. Establish consistent, easily remembered starting and ending hours for all days of registration.

A commercial bank sponsors a radio advertisement which ridicules its competitors for offering inconsistent service hours on various days of the week. In the advertisement the sponsor asks if the public is not confused by such hours as 9:00 a.m. to 2:00 p.m. on Mondays, Tuesdays, and Wednesdays, 9:30 a.m. to 3:30 p.m. on Thursdays, 9:00 a.m. to 2:00 p.m. and 4:00 p.m. to 6:00 p.m. on Fridays, and 10:00 a.m. to 1:00 p.m. on Saturdays.

The advertisement builds on existing confusion, and the bank solves the problem by stating a clear policy of being *open ten to six, six days a week.*

One community college has hours of 10:00 a.m. to 2:00 p.m. for preregistration, 9:00 a.m. to 3:00 p.m. and 6:00 p.m. to 7:30 p.m. for regular registration, and 10:00 a.m. to 2:00 p.m. and 6:30 p.m. to 8:00 p.m. for late registration. Even college employees forget when to report for duty!

Try to memorize the preceding paragraph, or type it, or read it aloud three times quickly. Then take action to simplify registration hours.

79. Offer registration on weekends and other times matching class scheduling.

Registration should be offered at any time and on any day of the week when classes are held. Students interested in a class held on Monday evenings should be allowed to register on a Monday evening. Saturday students should be allowed to register on a Saturday. Students interested in a 5:30 p.m. class should not be forced to register at 10:00 a.m. or 8:00 p.m.

Students select classes in part due to the appropriateness of the classes to their other schedule commitments. Registration limited to all day Wednesday and Thursday may conflict with the prospective student's availability on Tuesdays.

Saturday registration is recommended even if there are no weekend classes. Saturday registration is rather attractive among some persons who seem to need to complete their weekly obligations, relax, and enroll on their day off. Perhaps the other working spouse can take care of the children on the weekend, there may be only one automobile in the household to drive to registration, or it may be that part of Friday's paycheck is needed for registration.

For a variety of reasons, Saturday registration is usually very popular.

80. Provide a registration form center.

Near the registrar's or admissions offices there should be a rack with supplies of each enrollment form used by the institution. These forms should include admissions applications, re-admissions applications, registration forms, drop-add forms, transcript applications, and others. There should also be a supply of class schedules and a counter-top writing surface. Nearby there should be a lock box or a drop chute for students to submit completed forms. On a wall above the counter top instructions should be posted along with samples of properly completed forms.

Such a form center is valuable because the admissions or records office will not usually be open at all times when students and prospective students are on campus, especially in the evenings and on weekends. Also, the form center will reduce routine office traffic, and there are some students who prefer a self-service opportunity for simple procedures.

Many institutions wisely provide a stand containing brochures describing the various programs and services available. This stand should be near, but not combined with, the form center due to crowding of both documents and visitors. Seating should be provided for those who require reading time. A reading area will encourage students to ask questions on campus.

SECTION ELEVEN

INSTRUCTION

SECTION 11

81. Allow students to determine part of the content of special interest courses.

Potential students are more likely to enroll if there is a generally recognized policy of allowing students to determine part of the content of special interest courses such as Investments, History of Jazz, or Weaving.

Students of specialized adult learning topics bring unique priorities along with their keen interest and enthusiasm. Students of Real Estate Property Management, for example, might be interested in renting rooms in their homes, managing duplexes, or forming limited partnerships for large apartment projects. A class composed of persons interested in increasing the profitability of existing properties should not sit through too many lectures devoted to feasibility studies for new rental units.

Most course descriptions should end with ". . . and other topics of interest to the class."

82. Minimize term paper requirements.

Ten to fifteen years ago students could complete all requirements for a bachelor's degree at most colleges and universities without writing more than half a dozen term papers. Writing assignments were typically limited to writing courses. The current trend is to require a term paper for nearly every course, except for the sciences, mathematics, studio art and a few others.

A limitation in term paper requirements is necessary if an educational institution is to grow by attracting more new students from among local citizens in the 1980's, while numbers of high school graduates decline. Many new citizen-students are not capable writers and do not seek writing skills outside of writing courses. When required to write they either will not enroll or will write poorly, reinforcing errors. Instructors may associate lack of writing skill with lack of intelligence or learning progress. Nearly all instructors other than composition teachers will fail to make needed corrections.

The great body of effort in writing a term paper is devoted to preparation, editing, and typing—not learning. Oral reports generate recitation practice and apprehension, rather than knowledge—and often waste class time.

83. Make class assignments useful, not mere exercises.

One of the biggest flaws in teaching and one of the most significant deterrents to enrollment is the assignment of purely academic exercises. It is better to obtain evidence of student commitment and learning from useful projects. Productive activities can reinforce the importance of new knowledge, and through them students can be made to feel mature, involved, and valued.

Professorial passions for term papers can be redirected toward publishable articles, if only for the campus newspaper, neighborhood shoppers guide, or association newsletter. Accounting students can help keep accounts for campus clubs or citizen groups, rather than figure funds for fictitious firms.

Part of the excitement of teaching is to apply knowledge in a useful situation. There is no reason to deny useful applications to students.

84. Familiarize new part-time instructors with the instrument for student evaluation of instruction.

Great progress has been made over the past ten years in the development of instruments for student evaluation of instruction. Forms are now in common use which cover the instructor's preparation for class, clarity of learning objectives, attainment of objectives, delivery, mannerisms, and personal attention, to mention a few common questionnaire items. A well-designed form should be a useful guide for instruction, and most instructors should be familiar with its content.

Most part-time instructors first become aware of evaluation forms when forms appear in their mail boxes just prior to the last class meeting, or when they are distributed and collected in class by a student who has orders to withhold them from teachers.

New, or nearly new, instructors should be given the evaluation form in advance and have its criteria serve as a guide for successful teaching.

85. Allow students to make progress toward their educational goals.

A common complaint among freshman and sophomore students is that they devote too much time to survey courses, prerequisites, and general studies including Biology, Mathematics, Government, Psychology, History and English.

A work-study student in the author's office gave up a position in a local firm in order to prepare himself for supervision and management analysis. His grades, self-image, and interest in education were seriously damaged by lack of interest and ability in Biology, Sociology, and Literature. Not one course in his program of study seemed related to his learning and career goals.

Full-time students need to explore interests and sort out priorities through a varied academic schedule, but when little or no study moves them closer to the achievement of their goals, alternatives emerge such as transfer, military service, or jobs.

SECTION TWELVE

SPECIAL OPPORTUNITIES

SECTION 12

86. Offer concentrated courses between regularly scheduled semester or quarter terms.

It is a great advantage for some prospective students to complete prerequisites or other requirements, such as for career licensing, in a short time. Classes between the summer and fall terms (Pre-Fall or Summer Quick Quarter), and over the Christmas vacation (Winterim), are examples. A class which meets thirty hours can be held from 9 a.m. to 12 noon, and from 1 p.m. to 4 p.m. for five days, or over two weeks in the mornings or afternoons only.

Accelerated courses offer the educational institution the advantage of serving new students and of generating enrollment revenue at times when expenses continue, but income may be interrupted.

87. Offer adult education and early-college classes at all regional high schools.

Each high school is a community center well known to nearly every resident in its population area. Citizens are involved with each high school as parents, former students, attending students, and visitors for athletic events, precinct voting, or other special events. High schools provide familiar locations based on population which are attractive to many persons. High schools are usually free of forbidding academic pretense, and their locations can offer transportation cost savings to nearby citizens. Classes offered at high school sites should include topics suitable for the satisfaction of adult learning interests and for the accumulation of transferable college credits by high school students.

The college or university should expect to pay a small fee

for lighting, temperature control, and janitorial services. Such unexpected revenue is attractive to high school administrators because college use of high school classrooms creates no great additional expense. High school administrators will often welcome college courses in order to serve taxpayers, and to justify capital and maintenance outlays for buildings which might otherwise seem under-used on evenings and weekends.

Even the most reluctant high school administration will be more likely to cooperate if its principal or other staff member is paid a small annual fee to become coordinator of college activities.

There is seldom a good reason to omit any high school.

88. Use public libraries as learning centers.

Libraries have obvious attractions for persons interested in new information, skill building, and spare time enjoyment. Libraries frequently have meeting room space which can be used for classes. The central library in a city, county or region is located in consideration of population distribution, as are the often numerous branches. Library personnel are typically motivated to increase circulation and citizen participation as both a measure of their success and as justification for funding.

Given a library policy receptive to cooperative efforts with schools, colleges, and universities, it is common to find that members of the library staff are community leaders with influence among persons with knowledge acquisition habits. Librarians have keen insight into learning needs which require teaching supplement to books. A member of the library staff may be awarded an annual stipend as compensation for indentifying learning interests, recommending local experts for teaching, locating classroom space, and providing course notices to library visitors.

All libraries and branches should be approached for the

purpose of sponsoring instruction. Classes might be conducted in library facilities or at nearby locations recommended by the library staff. Such mutual public service endorsements will be a credit both to the public library and to the educational institution.

89. Establish sites for classes which draw on population centers in adjacent service areas.

State colleges, and especially community colleges, often have well-defined service area boundaries encompassing one or more cities or counties. One aggressive means to enrollment growth is to operate extension sites near the outer border of the institution's service area located to serve population centers on the other side of the line in the service area of another school.

Radio stations, television stations, and newspapers which serve both areas are unobtrusive means of publicity for such sites.

90. Offer instruction at correctional institutions, including local jails.

While course offerings at state prisons are not uncommon, local jails are often overlooked as instructional sites. A sizable population of inmates is often retained at local jails for several months or more due to overcrowding of prisons, the retention of persons at the jail for short-term convictions, and delays in pre-trial court actions.

Instruction at local jails, as well as prisons, should be recommended to correctional officers or their governing boards and agencies. Course content can be identified by those who serve as classification officers or counselors at the jail, and the days, times, and duration of instruction should be tailored to correctional facility routines. There will often be an Adult Basic Education (ABE) program at the jail or prison, and its graduates are likely students for more advanced study.

Jail and prison administrators will benefit from constructive activities within their walls, and local Offender Aid and Restoration (OAR) chapters can provide additional enthusiasm. Probation officers, too, might welcome college courses for inmates and can support "transfer" to full-time higher education upon release.

91. Offer classes at senior citizen centers and public housing projects.

Most communities are served by senior centers and public housing projects. What these two types of agencies have in common is that both typically offer planned recreational or self-improvement activities, and they both serve persons who might be thought of as members of subcultures, often needing increased ability to cope with well-defined and perceived problems.

Managers of public housing projects and senior citizen centers should be asked to study the feasibility of courses such as Child Care, Nutrition, Consumer Economics, Personal Health, and Aging, plus hobby courses such as Art and Music.

92. Encourage high school students to attend summer sessions or evening classes.

More high school students should be encouraged to sample their local college or university by attending summer sessions and evening classes.

This is not as much a call for innovation as for expansion. Surely there are few colleges or universities without high school students on their campuses each term for special courses. High school counselors have always steered the super scholars to collegiate excellence projects. The strict line between high school and higher education should be diminished for more students—perhaps twenty to thirty percent of high school juniors and seniors.

Part-time collegiate study can result in a savings of time and money for high school students and their families. Aside from increased tuition revenue, colleges and universities will have better opportunities to demonstrate their excellence and to increase their share of full-time students from among local high school graduates.

93. Open the college library to all area citizens.

One key to enrollment success is to attract as many citizens as possible to the campus for purposes other than registration. Having driven to the campus, found their way around, and become familiar with buildings and personnel, citizens are more likely to enroll in classes than if they had remained strangers to the institution.

Every local resident should be eligible for a library card and be allowed to check out books, borrow films and records, and have access to every other service of the library, including reference help. Library privileges should be publicized, not just available. Residents using the library should be given the opportunity to become acquainted with course offerings, and some will register. Goodwill could easily lead to the enrollment of family members and friends.

Special interest groups can be served, as in the case of Virginia community colleges which maintain teaching films and manikins in the libraries for the use of volunteer rescue squads. This resulted in large enrollments for Emergency Medical Training (EMT) classes at several institutions. Even more persons will be interested in the U.S. Internal Revenue Service (IRS) instructional tapes for income tax return preparation which can be obtained and made available. Citizens using the IRS tapes will be good prospects for related taxation courses.

Nearly every citizen who visits the institution will be surprised to meet neighbors and friends in the halls, and the contagious enthusiasm of sharing learning ideas will help boost enrollment.

94. Offer courses for shift workers at suitable times and sites.

Enrollment is built one student at a time, and there are readily identifiable career groups which can be served by courses offered shortly before or after shift employment hours. Industrial Management, Supervision, Health Care, Police Science, Hotel-Motel Management, Emergency Medical Training, and Fire Science are examples. Some courses can be taught at the work site, and even during work hours, as in the case of Fire Science.

Two or three shifts are common to many career specialties, usually ending at about midnight, 8 a.m., and 4 p.m. Shift work employees are often out of phase with normal retail and recreational attractions, so many will be receptive to study opportunities suited to their unique schedules.

SECTION THIRTEEN

FOLLOW-UP ACTIVITIES

SECTION 13

95. Plan to meet the learning needs of students for their entire lives, when consistent with institutional mission.

Many schools, colleges and university administrators seem to consider the student experience to be terminal, lasting only two to four years. It is assumed that every student must be replaced. An institution with a successful enrollment strategy will consider that it is building a life-long educational relationship with local students, as well as the students' families and friends.

Of course, in today's highly mobile society many students will leave the geographic area of the institution and cannot continue to be served. But even for those who stay, it is far more common to receive pleas for financial donations than to receive class schedules or other inducements to study. Even special alumni benefits, such as membership in a campus dining club, alumni stadium seats, and use of the college placement service, are offered in such a way as to identify former students as having outgrown student status.

Graduates may be sold university rocking chairs by mail order, may be invited to attend class reunions, or may be asked to assist with student recruitment. However, there is seldom an expectation that former students will return to the classroom in order to update skills, acquire new knowledge, prepare for career change, or plan for retirement. There is often an unexpressed opinion that those who return for study are in some way immature, or have failed to properly benefit from their student years.

The change required is one of attitude. Entering students are not the class of '84, but rather are assumed to have entered into a permanent educational relationship, including their own teaching role in some cases.

96. Implement a performance follow-up system.

Only a very small part of a performance follow-up system consists of research studies of former students. True performance follow-up is a continuing relationship with employees and employers to insure the best possible performance in the careers of former students.

Employers should be asked to evaluate former students with declining frequency over the years, and there should be annual awards from the school for former students who are highly evaluated or who achieve some other distinction such as very high salaries, promotion to supervisory status, or professional leadership.

Employers should enter into a performance commitment relationship with the school, and the school should provide class work to correct deficiencies. In these several ways the school builds pride among its former students, a demand for its graduates, and successful enrollment.

97. Send class schedules and priority registration forms to all local former students.

Former students, be they intermittent full-timers, occasional part-time students, or graduates, are the best prospects for enrollment in the local population. Each former student should receive a special class schedule and a personal registration appointment, or other registration priority.

A college with 5,000 part-time students each semester or quarter may serve 20,000 individuals over a three- to five-year period. As students come and go to meet learning needs as well as other demands on their time, the greatest possible convenience and encouragement must exist for re-enrollment. Enrollment success requires the frequent "recycling" of students, or the supply of new local students will some day reach scarcity, or even exhaustion.

SECTION FOURTEEN

PUBLIC INFORMATION

SECTION 14

98. Assess public information for reverse impact.

Public information such as press releases, public service announcements, employment vacancy notices, class schedules, catalogs, and posters should be studied in order to minimize the potential for reverse impact. In this procedure educators attempt to imagine as many negative interpretations as possible. Persons outside the college or university should assist in this work because educators can become isolated and lose perspective.

One good example of reverse impact is a publicity campaign which was planned by a community college in which the institution was to promote the theme "You have already paid three quarters of your tuition." Since 75 percent of the institution's expenses are paid from tax revenue, the public information officer was planning to seek increased enrollment by boasting a 75 percent discount, or an opportunity to recoup the 75 percent paid in taxes without benefit by local non-students. The reverse impact in this case would have been that the majority of taxpayers would have it called to their attention that they are making possible a large educational discount for others. Some citizens might begin to think of the public institution as an educational welfare department where participants are subsidized by non-participants.

Even student success stories can have negative interpretations, because each student's goal is not shared by everyone in the story's audience. A student who accepts an important position in a distant state may be viewed as a lost investment. Many citizens will not be able to identify with foreign language scholars or with graduates of a police science curriculum, regardless of the level of success achieved by the students.

The potential for reverse impact cannot be totally eliminated from public information, but negative interpretations can be anticipated and reduced.

99. Do not predict or announce problems.

Institutional leaders often are tempted to predict or report problems in order to achieve some important goal. Even when the goal is achieved, the negative impact of calling attention to problems can result in a net loss to the school.

For example, problem prediction often occurs when educators seek funding by predicting disastrous consequences if full funding is not received from local, state or federal governments. The predictions of professional layoffs and student application rejections take their toll on enrollment whether or not the desired level of funding is received. Some prospective students will decide to share their futures with another institution having its own bright future.

An example of problem publicity occurred when the normally crowded respiratory therapy program at one community college began to experience enrollment declines despite the great employment success of its graduates. In an attempt to rebuild enrollment demand college personnel printed posters and wrote press releases calling attention to vacancies and under-enrollment. Vacancy signs are fine for motels, but *vacancies* in successful curricula are *opportunities*. Readers of the publicity regarding respiratory therapy might have obtained the impression that the program had been abandoned by thoughtful students, when actually the enrollment declines were probably due to formerly high applicant rejection rates and the program's stature of exclusiveness.

100. Promote benefits other than learning.

Education is a desirable goal and there are millions of persons studying at postsecondary schools, colleges, and universities in order to obtain needed or desired knowledge and skills. Large numbers of non-students can be motivated to attend by a combination of incentives including fellowship, self-renewal, and prestige.

Fellowship is a strong motivation, and the institution can publicize art classes, for example, by portraying the campus as a center for beginning and accomplished artists—a sort of art club.

Nearly everyone seems to feel a need for self-renewal, self-expression, and an enrichment of their personal and professional lives. Courses such as Decision Making, Career Strategies, Retirement Planning, Human Relations, and Assertiveness Training should be promoted with an emphasis on perceptions and attitudes in addition to knowledge to be gained.

Many national magazines and newspapers are advertised with an appeal to a prospective reader's desire for advancement, financial advantage, and popularity. The reader's subscription is said to lead to wise investments, better conversations, increased admiration by friends and colleagues, and multi-rung leaps up the ladder of success.

Human beings seem to have a pack instinct. Most want to be in style and not miss out on anything others are enjoying. Clothiers will tell us that hats are coming back, or that "every one is wearing orange this year." Jogging and Vitamin C are also "the rage." So don't be left out—everybody is going to college these days!

101. Advertise instructional results in addition to content and resources.

When manufacturers or retailers advertise a product, the public usually knows or is told the item's uses or advantages. A microwave oven can cook meals quickly, reduce electricity use, and produces little heat loss. Color television sets provide color pictures, and water spray devices can clean between

teeth. The manufacturer almost never describes the qualifications of its design engineers, details of construction, or its
own corporate strength.

Schools, colleges, and universities give great attention to
institutional stature, staff qualifications, and course content.
They seldom describe what it is that instruction in a course or
a curriculum will do for the student. For example, prospective students of Creative Writing will typically be told that the
college is accredited, that the instructor has a master's degree,
and that the course includes grammar, paragraphing, writing
practice, and corrections by the instructor. Publicity focused
on results would stress the ability to complete a publishable
manuscript, to design a manuscript for one or more specific
publishers, to identify and develop interesting content, and
to negotiate effectively with publishers for fees and copy-
rights.

102. Adopt a distinctive, attractive name and address.

With only about 3,000 colleges and universities in the
United States there seems little need for name duplication.
Yet, there are six Saint Pauls, thirty Saint Marys, eight Notre
Dames, and four Marymounts. More than thirty institutions
are known as "South" or "Southern" outside South Carolina
and South Dakota. One state college system has a nearly
indistinguishable set of prison-sounding names such as
Central State, East Central State, Northeastern State, South-
eastern State, and Southwestern State. There are also silly
sounding names like Slick Stream College, or Gopher
Canyon University. Some schools have names which confuse
their location, such as Minnesota College of Colorado, or San
Francisco University of Wyoming. Northern Community
College in one state is south of a sister institution, and Southwestern Community College is northeast of several others.

In 1978-79 more than fifty colleges and universities introduced name changes as listed in the college and university directory of the National Center for Educational Statistics. It can be done!

Addresses can also present unnecessary marketing problems. A neighboring post office can be used to avoid names like Webbs Cave, Wilderness, Gulch, Minnow Rapids, Mold, or Lizard Ridge. A mailing address can be changed to another corner of the campus to avoid street addresses such as Opossum Road or Asylum Avenue.

If the highway sign near your school reads something like "No Cty St Voc Tech Inst," try to have it improved.

THE BEST IDEAS FROM
THE ENROLLMENT WORKBOOK*

*Share Publishing Company, 1978

SECTION 15

103. Accept responsibility for enrollment.

Enrollment is important to the financial success of the institution and the optimism of its staff, and enrollment can be controlled.

The first step to increased enrollment is to accept responsibility for enrollment. External factors beyond the institution's control must not be blamed for low enrollment. These external excuses include the energy crisis, the declining birthrate, the end of the draft, Veterans' Administration changes, inflation, and the weather.

All administrators, teachers, librarians, secretaries, and groundskeepers must understand that their actions and decisions control enrollment. Enrollment is not an accident.

Not only are enrollment statistics usually the basis for institutional funding; enrollment also strongly influences the pride, morale, and enthusiasm of educators. Low enrollment causes doubts about the worth of service provided. Ambition can erode among educators working in what seems to be a dying organization.

104. Write an enrollment plan, including what must be done and by whom.

In order to increase enrollment there must be institutional change and a plan for making changes. The plan should contain numerous steps, such as adding new courses or increasing advertising. Most of the recommendations in this book could become steps in an enrollment plan. The written plan should also designate the person responsible for implementation, a date for completion, and some way to determine whether the action had the desired result.

The plan need not be a bureaucratic exercise. It can be quite simple and informal. The enrollment plan need not even be typed or copied as long as there is a consensus and a commitment. For example, the registrar might simply agree to longer registration hours, or the public information specialist might be given funds for a bulk mailing of class schedules to each household in the area.

105. Provide a problem table during registration.

A special table at registration should be designated "Special Problems." This table is a last resort, a last hope, for students with the most frustrating problems. Administrators, faculty, or clerical personnel should be present at all times. Only the most knowledgeable and helpful persons should be considered for the problem table assignment.

The problem table will be enormously popular with students, and great fun for workers at the table.

106. Compensate for registration surge.

Students hate lines at registration, as you know from having been a student. Some potential students will just walk away. Some will see it through, but will not come back, or will tell their friends not to bother. The most common cause of lines is surge. Students pile up at one station after another while other stations are temporarily empty. Surge can best be cured by registration appointments. One university in Florida sends each returning student or admitted student a card with an exact registration appointment. This may be too expensive and complicated for the small institution and does little to help walk-in students, who are exactly the students needed to build local enrollments.

Two other cures for surge are cheap and easy. The first is to have a different starting time for registration than that announced. If the published starting time of registration is

10:00 a.m., a crowd will gather at 9:30 and grow rapidly. Once the floodgates are opened at 10:00, the surge will cause lines at each station in turn for the next hour or so. The obvious solution is to begin registration at 9:30. So easy; so rare. Some students will gradually learn to come early, but new students, who are necessary for institutional growth, will not. The other solution is to have comprehensively trained registration workers who can move from one overworked station to another.

107. Offer registration by mail or by phone.

Many registrars will tell you that mail and telephone registration is impossible. Others do not know there is any other way. At one campus on the East Coast, noncredit students register by mail or by telephone, but credit students may not.

A combination telephone-and-mail registration for persons taking only one or two courses should be attempted. Students are invited to telephone and are asked their name and address and the course or courses desired. Each student is sent the necessary forms with the understanding that the forms and payment for the course must be returned within a certain period. Spaces are reserved for callers until their reply period expires.

Once the institution gains experience with a limited telephone-and-mail registration, it may wish to expand this service. Is walk-in registration so pleasant, inexpensive, accurate, and quick that it can never be replaced?

108. Eliminate nuisance fees.

The manner in which services are priced and the method by which fees are collected in education is inconsistent with practices in nearly all other trades, businesses, and professions.

The special fees charged by educational institutions discourage enrollment because they are perceived as an added tax over and above the true value of the instructional service paid for in the regular tuition. One college with serious enrollment problems charges an admission fee of fifteen dollars, a student activity fee of three dollars, an athletic fee of two dollars, and a late registration fee of ten dollars. Total fees are between twenty and thirty dollars, which is nearly as great as tuition for one credit. The fees offer no value to the student taking a night course in income tax preparation or creative writing. Assuming that the fees are essential to the institution, they would better be included in tuition, where they would accurately reflect the cost of operating the school and offering instruction.

109. Feature courses and curricula in catalogs and schedules.

The first page and even the cover of a Sears Roebuck catalog feature merchandise the firm offers for sale. Nothing precedes the merchandise, because the Sears catalog is a merchandising publication. A typical college or university catalog will feature its logo, members of the board, members of the administration, members of the faculty, a history of the institution, its purpose, accreditation, admission requirements, residency rules, student classifications, and scores of other discouraging pages.

Why does Sears not print in its catalog the names and pictures of its President and Board of Directors, or the history of Sears, or a classification of different types of customers? Because such information does not sell merchandise.

110. Publish an annual schedule of classes.

This is merely a suggestion to let potential students know what to expect in advance. Advance planning can result in sequential enrollment rather than mass turnover. An ambitious bank teller might be more likely to sign up for a fall course on Bank Operations if the teller also knows that Analyzing Financial Statements and Bank Accounting will follow. The three courses would be a greater asset than the one. For some students the three-course package would be more attractive than one course, and the follow-up courses could actually provide the motivation for taking the first course.

111. Counsel all prospective students without appointments.

The potential student who walks into the college must not be handed a catalog, given an appointment, and sent away. When a person takes the time and makes the effort to approach the institution, it is a ripe moment to provide a positive influence. The visitor is motivated and receptive. On the other hand, half an hour alone at home with the catalog and five days of waiting for an interview can be very discouraging. Surely there must be one counselor, one administrator, or one teacher who can take a few minutes to say hello and talk about the institution and the visitor. A complete follow-up interview can be scheduled for a later date if appropriate.

The visitor who is sent away may visit another institution, may send away for information out of state, or may just give up on education. Some persons actually fear a scheduled interview.

112. Assign an educational planner to each part-time student.

The counseling and advising offered to most part-time students is inadequate. The institution must provide mentors whose job is not simply to teach or keep the paperwork flowing, but also to guide, support, and encourage part-time students.

A middle-aged student wants to improve job possibilities, sees a course listed in the newspaper called "Shorthand Refresher," walks in, signs up, finishes the course, and walks out. What about Business Machines, or Legal Terminology, or Data Processing? These courses would provide more job skills the student may need. The shorthand refresher course might not have been the appropriate stenographic course for this student. Who knows? Who cares?

113. Take pains to see that students register in courses well suited to their abilities and interests.

Many of the students who drift away after one course or one semester were simply in the wrong classes. About three-quarters of the way through regular registration and throughout late registration on thousands of campuses, one can see students groping through schedules and checking cancellation boards looking for two more credits, or something on Thursday afternoon. Counselors are tired, students are numb, and a fine-arts major signs up for dairy goat management because it meets after the part-time job and someone said there is no term paper.

The student, who has no background in animal husbandry, takes the course, does poorly, and complains loudly, never mentioning to friends and family any satisfaction with the other three courses taken.

114. Offer in-class early registration.

Toward the end of the semester or quarter, students should be thinking about which courses to take next; but they usually are behind in assignments or worried about exams, and before they know it, they are dropouts.

The instructor, a counselor, or an administrator should take fifteen minutes out of one of the final class meetings to talk with the class about related courses to be offered next session. The new class schedule can be distributed along with special early registration forms. Students can complete the forms and pay tuition in the classroom, or they can register at a special advance registration day to follow.

115. Keep records of all employer contacts, agreements, and services.

Confusion is a common problem in an institution's attempt to conduct employer training. Consider the number of institutional representatives who may haphazardly interact with employers. The placement officer contacts employers regarding graduates or other former students seeking permanent employment. The Financial Aid Office may place students in part-time jobs. The Business Division head may contact the employer in recruiting part-time faculty from among the firm's executives. The Development Office may seek financial support.

No coherent favorable image of the educational institution is likely to emerge from this unorganized pattern of contacts. One administrator should be designated coordinator of employer relations and be asked to keep a set of simple records, including (1) a general description of the employer, its product or service, and its staff; (2) past training experience with the employer; and (3) any contacts with employers, especially those involving requests and commitments.

116. Cultivate positive working relationships with the news media.

Schools, colleges, and universities should build positive working relationships with the news media by appointing editors, writers, announcers, and others to teach courses such as Journalism, Radio-Television Production, and Advertising. Cooperative ventures by the institution and the media can include courses by radio, television and newspaper. The news media may also be represented on institutional governing boards and advisory committees.

Of course, all institutions should supply the media with press releases and public service announcements. Newspapers often receive criticism for not providing adequate local coverage and may welcome well-written real news. Radio and television stations have a license obligation to become involved in community affairs.

117. Send targeted mailings of course posters.

Targeted mailings are the best advertising. One-page posters are attractive and informative. They can be produced for any course needing promotion and mailed to persons who might be inclined to enroll in the course. For example, a mailing describing a citizens' course in nuclear energy and radiation safety can be sent to all physicians, dentists, hospitals, hospital supply firms, physicists, engineers, and environmental groups. A horse science poster can be mailed to stables, tack shops, western shops, feed stores, tractor dealers, riding clubs, farms and extension agents.

Several courses can be mentioned on one poster when the courses are closely related, but long lists will lose the reader's attention and defeat the purpose of a targeted mailer.

118. Conduct poster trips in the community.

Another batch of posters can be tacked or taped all over campus and all over town. Some good places to display posters are libraries, post offices, bus stations, airports, barber shops, beauty salons, bookstores, department stores, supermarket bulletin boards, and City Hall. Always ask permission and return to remove posters. It is also great fun to post notices at competing institutions.

Specific locations can be matched to individual courses just as in the case of targeted mailings. A poster on a weaving course, for example, can be posted in hobby shops and fabric stores.

ENROLLMENT STRATEGY CHECK LIST

SECTION 16

Enrollment Strategy Check List

Number	Suggestion	Present Use Score	Assigned To	Target Date
1. Rate each administrative activity according to its enrollment growth potential.				
2. Establish a clear sense of mission and market position.				
3. Keep records of the amount of time devoted to enrollment producing activities.				
4. Make expenditure decisions on the basis of how much enrollment revenue each dollar will return.				
5. Give revenue producers greater influence over institutional policy than is held by revenue-dependent personnel.				
6. Make decisions regarding buildings and grounds on the basis of enrollment return.				
7. Appoint an enrollment committee and/or enrollment coordinator.				
8. Do not initiate new fees or inflate fees when increases in services or in participation would better increase revenue.				

Number	Suggestion	Present Use Score	Assigned To	Target Date
9. Determine the number of service area high school graduates, where such persons study in higher education, and the institution's enrollment share.				
10. Study prospective students who visit, write for information, apply, or are admitted, but do not enroll.				
11. Determine why some students select the institution and enroll.				
12. Conduct research on public knowledge and perceptions of the institution.				
13. Study competing institutions to determine their advantages and disadvantages.				
14. Obtain data on the enrollment success of academic units and personnel.				
15. Obtain management data on trends in enrollment by race, sex, credit hour load, subject area, age, term enrolled, etc.				
16. Determine instructional needs and interests by offering courses, rather than through interest surveys.				
17. Study commercial markets in an effort to identify productive extension sites.				
18. Use data in management decisions in order to make changes.				
19. Require all professional personnel to make an enrollment contribution.				

Number	Suggestion	Present Use Score	Assigned To	Target Date
20. Award larger salaries and larger increases to enrollment productive administrators.				
21. Award benefits to enrollment productive administrators, such as extra vacation time, better budgets, larger staffs, less committee work, or more travel.				
22. Award promotions and other benefits to faculty with large classes.				
23. Provide customer relations training for all institutional personnel.				
24. Other credentials being equal, give priority in employment to persons with retail business experience.				
25. Conceal internal disputes from the public and news media.				
26. Subdue personal causes, religion, politics, etc.				
27. Provide an obvious reception area for prospective students and other new visitors.				
28. Post direction signs showing the way to counselors, the community services office, and others.				
29. Assign functional names to college buildings which can be understood by non-students.				
30. Do not isolate administrators from visiting citizens, students and prospective students.				

Number	Suggestion	Present Use Score	Assigned To	Target Date
31.	Do not screen telephone calls, ask the names of callers, or the nature of their calls.			
32.	Be certain that all buildings, grounds, equipment, and furnishings are orderly, clean, and in good repair.			
33.	Make class schedules simple, brief and uncluttered.			
34.	Avoid reliance on newspaper insert course announcements.			
35.	Repeat course publicity in various forms and at various times in order to gain maximum coverage and to achieve reinforcement through repetition.			
36.	Publish only one alphabetical sequence of classes in the course schedule and do not categorize classes by time or location.			
37.	Provide an alphabetical index of classes if departmental or other groupings make classes difficult to find.			
38.	Avoid confusing abbreviations.			
39.	Publish pictures and biographies of counselors and other public contact personnel.			
40.	Display exhibits of student learning in order to stimulate course interest.			
41.	Use a focus board or enlarged type size to call attention to enrollment-building classes.			

Number	Suggestion	Present Use Score	Assigned To	Target Date
42. Provide recorded telephone messages on courses, programs, and registration details.				
43. Insure that all public announcements and correspondence support enrollment goals.				
44. Identify professional personnel in order to invite inquiries concerning the institution.				
45. Provide college plaques for the offices of successful part-time instructors.				
46. Provide signs to personnel offices in recognition of training projects.				
47. Distribute institutional reminders such as catalogs, class schedules, conference folders, and calendars to visitors and other citizens.				
48. Give recognition to sponsors of special events.				
49. Offer a wide range of student activities for the pursuit of special interests and the development of leadership skills.				
50. Award student leaders grants in support of student activities.				
51. Promote activities for part-time students.				
52. Assist youth groups in the attainment of their goals.				
53. Encourage prestige transfer.				

Number	Suggestion	Present Use Score	Assigned To	Target Date
54. Hold an annual reception or party for the families of enrolled students.				
55. Provide convenient, responsive channels for student complaints and suggestions.				
56. Rotate the time, day, and location of special interest courses each term.				
57. Investigate career certification and licensing requirements in order to offer appropriate training.				
58. Do not cancel small classes of eight or more students.				
59. Avoid image-destroying courses.				
60. Offer numerous educational opportunities on weekends.				
61. Ask students in class which course topics interest them for subsequent semesters or quarters.				
62. Analyze the class schedule each term prior to its publication in order to insure sufficient enrollment capacity.				
63. Corroborate employer advice on new courses and programs.				
64. Give attention to forecasting or futurism in order to take advantage of learning interests concerning changes in government, natural resources, economics, demographics, and culture.				

Number	Suggestion	Present Use Score	Assigned To	Target Date
65.	Inform adjunct faculty members that part of their assignment is to promote their courses.			
66.	Sponsor a regional job and educational opportunity fair.			
67.	Place college and university information at tourist centers.			
68.	Establish a campus travelers attraction or tourists information center.			
69.	Offer campus activities for local students visiting home from distant institutions.			
70.	Invite local prospective students to attend visitors class sessions.			
71.	Videotape counselors and others as they conduct admissions interviews.			
72.	Encourage counselors and advisors to refer students and prospective students to colleagues.			
73.	Invite families and friends of prospective students to admissions interviews when there is to be a shared decision.			
74.	Allow prospective students to enroll at the time of admissions interviews or pre-enrollment counseling.			
75.	Make student parking spaces available to visitors during registration, as well as meals and other conveniences.			

Number	Suggestion	Present Use Score	Assigned To	Target Date
76.	Insure that at least one half of the teaching faculty is on campus during all times of registration.			
77.	Inform all registration workers immediately of canceled classes, filled classes, and especially new classes and sections.			
78.	Establish consistent, easily remembered starting and ending hours for all days of registration.			
79.	Offer registration on weekends and other times matching class scheduling.			
80.	Provide a registration form center.			
81.	Allow students to determine part of the content of special interest courses.			
82.	Minimize term paper requirements.			
83.	Make class assignments useful, not mere exercises.			
84.	Familiarize new part-time instructors with the instrument for student evaluation of instruction.			
85.	Allow students to make progress toward their educational goals.			
86.	Offer concentrated courses between regularly scheduled semester or quarter terms.			
87.	Offer adult education and early-college classes at all regional high schools.			

Number	Suggestion	Present Use Score	Assigned To	Target Date
88. Use public libraries as learning centers.				
89. Establish sites for classes which draw on population centers in adjacent service areas.				
90. Offer instruction at correctional institutions, including local jails.				
91. Offer classes at senior citizen centers and public housing projects.				
92. Encourage high school students to attend summer sessions or evening classes.				
93. Open the college library to all area citizens.				
94. Offer courses for shift workers at suitable times and sites.				
95. Plan to meet the learning needs of students for their entire lives, when consistent with institutional mission.				
96. Implement a performance follow-up system.				
97. Send class schedules and priority registration forms to all local former students.				
98. Assess public information for reverse impact.				
99. Do not predict or announce problems.				

Number	Suggestion	Present Use Score	Assigned To	Target Date
100. Promote benefits other than learning.				
101. Advertise instructional results in addition to content and resources.				
102. Adopt a distinctive, attractive name and address.				
103. Accept responsibility for enrollment.				
104. Write an enrollment plan, including what must be done and by whom.				
105. Provide a problem table during registration. 106. Compensate for registration surge.				
107. Offer registration by mail or by phone.				
108. Eliminate nuisance fees.				
109. Feature courses and curricula in catalogs and schedules.				
110. Publish an annual schedule of classes.				
111. Counsel all prospective students without appointments.				
112. Assign an educational planner to each part-time student.				
113. Take pains to see that students register in courses well suited to their abilities and interests.				

Number	Suggestion	Present Use Score	Assigned To	Target Date
114. Offer in-class early registration.				
115. Keep records of all employer contacts, agreements, and services.				
116. Cultivate positive working relationships with the news media.				
117. Send targeted mailings of course posters.				
118. Conduct poster trips in the community.				

SECTION SEVENTEEN

CASE STUDY

SECTION 17

Case Study

In May, 1980, the author made a brief study of the enrollment strategy at a community college in Virginia. The results
illustrate some important lessons.

Beginning with the summer quarter 1980 the institution
increased its tuition rate. While the increase was small and
was dictated by state-wide policy, the increase harms chances
for enrollment success and violates suggestion Number 8 on
not inflating fees. The number of courses and sections were
reduced from last summer in several categories such as
music, marketing, photography, and others. This may have
resulted from an attempt to control faculty payroll expenditures and violates suggestion Number 4 on giving priority to
expenditures based on potential revenue production, and
suggestion Number 62 on insuring sufficient courses and
sections to achieve enrollment success.

The cover of the summer class schedule was illustrated
with drawings of garden vegetables. There were no garden-
ing classes in the list of courses, and the college offers no
agriculture programs. The vegetables may have been appropriate for the cover of a seed catalog, but their use in the class
schedule violates suggestion Number 2 on establishing a
sense of mission and image, and suggestion Number 109 on
featuring courses in catalogs and course schedules.

There were no out-reach course locations, in contrast with
past years, violating suggestion Number 87 and others in
section Twelve. A coding system used to identify the sponsoring department of each course was changed so that the Business Technologies division was represented by the letter "G"

rather than "B" and Continuing Education was changed from "C" to "M," thus violating suggestion Number 38 on avoiding confusing abbreviations.

Institutional leaders had planned to inaugurate a telephone-and-mail registration procedure for the summer quarter, but its cancellation resulted in the violation of suggestion Number 107 concerning telephone and mail registration.

The schedule of classes contained a statement of policy preventing students from dropping or adding classes after registration unless they provide copies of their original registration forms or previous drop-add forms. Most such copies are lost or are given to parents or employers who pay tuition, thus discouraging students from adding classes. The policy could also encourage students to stay in classes for which they have lost enthusiasm. Any unnecessary obstacle to adding classes violates the spirit of the entire section on Registration, and an obstacle to changing classes violates suggestion Number 113 on taking pains to see that students register in courses suited to their abilities and interests in order to avoid disappointment.

A $5.00 fine for returned checks is prominently listed in the class schedule in violation of suggestion Number 108 on eliminating nuisance fees, and suggestions Number 98 and 109 on avoiding negative statements in catalogs, class schedules, and other public information. An educational institution has eight weeks or more to collect a bad debt; it is not as if a customer has escaped with a television set. Overdrawn checking accounts usually result from innocent errors and educators should realize that students are at the institution to develop skills, rather than to exhibit skills. A friendly letter or short-term loan will solve the problem in nearly all cases.

This is a very brief report on one institution, and we know of many other suggestions in this book which are not in use there. For example, there is no enrollment coordinator (Number 7), there are few rewards for enrollment success (Number 20), there is no customer relations training (23), and there are far fewer course posters than in previous years (117, 118).

Finally, the summer 1980 schedule did not contain the institution's address or telephone number!

On the positive side, educators at this college have built very successful relationships with the news media (suggestion Number 116). For example, summer 1980 publicity was boosted by a five-part "closer look" series on a radio station. The series described the institution in highly complimentary terms, with segments of the series repeated several times each day during a week-long period. The report was written and presented by one of the station's newscasters *who had been hired part-time by the college to teach tennis.*

Similarly, the college provides a softball field for a radio station's team which plays other teams sponsored by community service groups, with the proceeds from game tickets going to worthy causes. Members of the radio station's team are its announcers and disc jockeys who promote the games on the air with great frequency and enthusiasm. They call themselves the "Ducks" and repeatedly refer to *their Duck Stadium at . . . College.* When games are scheduled with newspaper-sponsored teams or those of other radio stations there is an almost inescapable saturation of publicity by all media. Constructive involvement with most media editors, writers, and announcers is of priceless value.

Administrators at the institution conducted a very successful research study of public perceptions and attitudes concerning the college (suggestion Number 12). One of the findings was that many citizens considered themselves too old for college enrollment, and publicity followed which called attention to the majority of students at the institution who were not in the so-called college age group of 18 to 23 years.

The college also has a very well designed self-service registration form center (suggestion Number 80), and a walk-in counseling booth is occasionally available (suggestion Number 111).